Habakkuk,
The Man with
Honest Questions

Habakkuk, The Man with Honest Questions

Walter J. Ungerer

CONTEMPORARY DISCUSSION SERIES

BAKER BOOK HOUSE
Grand Rapids, Michigan

This study could not have been made without the help and support of many fellow sojourners. I am thankful to my wife, Janet, who never let me lose sight of the desire to write. I am also grateful to Baker Book House for their encouragement.

I am indebted to my secretaries past and present, Mable Hoody and Betty Ojala, for typing notes and revisions, and to Ronnie Huber, who volunteered to type the final manuscript.

I am grateful to a host of others who made suggestions and helped to develop the discussion questions: Marge Adams, Joan Baden, Sharon Brevik, Phyllis Davies, Barb Smyth, Mary Grace Thomas, and Herb Wewer.

I appreciate the support of the membership and staff of the Northfield Presbyterian Church who granted me the time to write and encouraged me to seek publication.

ISBN: 0-8010-9202-7

To

CLARA RUTH STONE

teacher, friend, encourager

and to

the other faculty members of

The Northeastern Bible College

who made the prophets live

PREFACE

During the period of time it has taken to put these thoughts in order, I have often been asked, "Habakkuk who?" "Is that really in the Bible?" "Why did you pick him?"

Let me answer these inquiries by stating that my interest in the Old Testament prophets goes back many years to my student days at the Northeastern Bible College located near Caldwell, New Jersey. It was there that I began my theological training and it was there through dedicated teachers that a deep reverence and appreciation for the prophets were kindled. Although their theory of interpretation and approach was more in keeping with the Dispensational school of thought (an approach I do not now myself maintain), these men made the prophets live.

As I took to reading these men of old privately they began to come alive one by one and seemed to come right out of the pages of Holy Writ. There were times when I felt as if Isaiah and Jeremiah were standing in my room. In a very real sense they do live, for whenever preachers of the Word allow the Biblical traditions of the prophets to permeate their ministry and lifestyle, men such as Isaiah and Jeremiah, Ezekiel and Daniel, do walk down the aisle of their churches and out into the streets of their communities and into the byways of the nation. This is a time in the history of America when the warnings of the prophets are sorely needed.

Of all the prophets, however, Habakkuk has become my favorite. It is not because he is easy to understand but because he says so much with such honesty and forethought, and speaks so forcefully in just a few short pages. I have developed a certain empathy with him for I too have on numerous occasions raised the same questions. I too have gotten angry with the Lord God. I too have walked that lonely path of despair and found the Lord of life walking alongside me. I too have found the same answers that gave Habakkuk his peace.

I am deeply indebted to a saint of another generation for introducing me to Habakkuk. It was Dr. Joseph G. Snyder, pastor for over fifty years of the Olivet Presbyterian Church of Brooklyn, New York, who, years after his death, opened the heart of this prophet to me. While a student at Northeastern I became student pastor of this little church which had become an inner city parish too poor to support a full-time pastor. Dr. Snyder died while serving the church and many of his papers and sermons were still in the files. One day while going through some of these files I came across a published monograph written by him in 1905 entitled, "Habakkuk, a Man with Questions." It was this small, little-known booklet about a little-known prophet that began a friendship which has lasted these many years. From that point on I began to take notes, to jot down things that came to mind, and the result is this book.

My intention is not to exhaust the exegetical content nor to make it so profound that the central theme gets lost, but rather to simply share the prophet's struggle and his hope with the ordinary layman, the man in the pew who also struggles like us pastors for answers and a clearer understanding of his faith.

One final word. I firmly believe that in Jesus Christ God fulfills all of the prophet's expectation and that Christ as Lord of life brings the kind of peace that Habakkuk came to know. For this reason I quickly move to the New Testament to explain or illustrate Habakkuk's problems. Without the light of the New Testament one cannot understand completely the Old Testament, and without the Old Testament one cannot understand completely the truth of the New Testament.

Contents

Contents

Introduction

Since Habakkuk is one of the prophets often lost in the archives of the Old Testament, unfortunately few of us are acquainted with the man and his message. In this obscure book we find such well-known statements as: "The just shall live by faith" (2:4); "The earth shall be filled with the knowledge of the glory of the Lord" (2:14); and "The Lord is in His holy temple; let all the earth keep silence before Him" (2:20).

Like other prophetic voices echoing from the pages of the Old Testament, Habakkuk is quite contemporary and his message is not only relevant but also necessary for our times, necessary for believers and nonbelievers alike. I am reminded of what Dr. Calkins said in his book, *The Modern Message of the Minor Prophets:*

Because the sins, social and personal, which the prophets condemn are root and essence the same as those which still degrade the soul of man and of society; because the truths which have their source in the holiness and justice of God are immutable and eternal; because the way of repentance and of a return to God's Word and will remains the only hope of redemption and of salvation therefore the inspired message of these prophets are not for their time only but for our time and for all time.

It cannot be said better and I agree; Habakkuk's message is especially necessary for Christians who are trying to understand the life of faith. I say this because, unfortunately, it is often true that Christians pay more attention to contemporary voices in areas of philosophy and literature than to the prophetic voice of Scripture. Needless to say, we cannot and should not ignore our contemporaries, but I believe that many times the Bible speaks even more candidly and forcefully to the issues that face us and as Christians we must come face to face with that fact.

To illustrate: Huxley in his novel, *Brave New World,* sees the danger of an overpopulated earth. His prophecy of an issue we are facing suggests that this crisis will lead to an unhealthy and dangerous consequence—the unavoidable creation of a rigid system of life. Eventually, a society will develop which will slowly take freedoms away until the individual is a slave of the state. Huxley's insight is a warning which suggests that, unless man is able to find a means to deal with this problem, he is doomed to slavery. Yet although Huxley is able to warn, he is unable to suggest a solution.

Another contemporary, Golding, in *Lord of the Flies,* depicts through the behavior of children on a desolate island the depravity of human life. But he leaves his reader with little hope to overcome the carnivorous, innate savagery of man. In contrast, the prophets of the Old Testament deal with known problems and direct us to their solution.

Before we go further, it might be wise to clear the air concerning the Old Testament prophets. They have been many times misunderstood. I believe it is heresy to assume that the prophets were simply crystal ball gazers or foretellers. Far from that—they were men of God directed by His Spirit who spoke of faith, hope and love. They were also led to speak forcefully and with deep conviction concerning the social conditions of their times. They were led to warn of devastation and chaos, of the choice between war and peace, moral and immoral practices.

J. Elliott Corbet in his book *The Prophets on Main Street* comments:

> *Their purpose as instruments of God was to redeem rather than to proclaim judgment. They wanted their people to turn from sin rather than reap the consequences of their disobedience. They brooded over the people and wept over resistant spirits. . . . They were often despised, sometimes feared, but always respected. What they had said proved upon the reflections of later generations to be true.*

Because I too maintain these convictions, I believe Habakkuk's message takes on great contemporary meaning. It is not so much prediction as it is a message of hope that God spoke through Habakkuk to a sinful, suffering people living on the brink of hell in every respect of their life.

Habakkuk, the Man—Who Is He?

First let it be said that there are some who express the opinion that Habakkuk was not an authentic person, that his name is a symbolic designation, as is thought to be the case with the prophet Malachi. Whether this can be substantiated or not, the name *Habakkuk* itself is of interest. It is thought that the origin of the name comes from the root *habak* which means "to caress," "to embrace," "to fold the hands." Because of this Martin Luther thought Habakkuk was a proper name for a prophet. It indicated that he was one who would take a problem to heart and become deeply concerned about it, or who would cling in desperation to his God. This, of course, is what Habakkuk does. He is deeply concerned for his times and clings to his God for an answer.

I am personally satisfied with the belief that Habakkuk was a real person and that he lived in Judah while she was passing through some of the darkest hours of her history. Some scholars are also of the opinion that Habakkuk was one of those special temple prophets who possessed great lyrical skills. The literary style suggests this since many see the book as a majestic hymn to Jehovah God. The closing remarks indicate that a choir should sing accompanied by string instruments (3:19).

In all likelihood his prophecy took place sometime between 600 and 598 B.C. when Jehoiakim was king of Judah. Jehoiakim was made king after the death of King Josiah and the short three month reign of Jehoahaz (II Kings 23:28-37). Jehoiakim was an evil ruler and reaped the fruits of an unjust reign. It was a time of chaos and frustration, national deterioration and political conflict.

I suggest for those interested in pursuing this period of history further that the *History of Israel* by John Bright, chapter 8, would be helpful. Also, the reading of II Kings 21—25 and Jeremiah 21, 26—29, 36—40, will give some indication of the stress and turmoil of Habakkuk's times. I will say something further about this matter later. But I can simply say here that Habakkuk was concerned with events at the end of the seventh century and the beginning of the sixth, when the Assyrians had fallen from power and the Babylonians (Chaldeans) were on the rise.

In the following pages we will look at the message of this prophet who relates how he was able to rise above and triumph over the conditions and the surroundings that threatened his life and that of his contemporaries. I am convinced that he can help us to understand our own times and our relationship with God who has revealed Himself in Jesus Christ. He will also give us hope for the times in which we live. For me no other prophet said it so well.

How many times must a man look up
    before he sees the sky?
And how many ears must one man have
    before he can hear people cry?
How many deaths will it take before we know
    that too many people have died?
The answer, my friend, is blowin' in the wind.
The answer is blowin' in the wind.

How many years can a mountain exist,
        before it is washed to the sea?
How many years can people exist
        before they long to be free?
How many times can a man turn his head
        and pretend he just doesn't see?
The answer my friend, is blowin' in the wind,
The answer is blowin' in the wind.

How many times must a man look up
        before he sees the sky?
And how many ears must one man have
        before he can hear people cry?
How many deaths will it take before we know
        that too many people have died?
The answer, my friend, is blowin' in the wind,
The answer is blowin' in the wind.

From "Blowin' in the Wind"

1. Habakkuk's Problem
Habakkuk 1:1-4

"Oh Lord: How long shall I cry and you will not hear me? Even when I cry unto you of violence you will not save. Why do you show me iniquity and cause me to behold grievance?" (1:2-3a).

How long and why? Here is an honest question from a man who has come face to face with life and all its realities, and what he sees he does not like, let alone understand. The prophet is a man sitting in darkness pleading for some kind of release. What caused him to cry out and what caused his despair? Why is he so frustrated with life?

His problem is to be found in his description of the iniquity of his times and God's delay in punishing it. Habakkuk sees firsthand the agonizing consequences of oppression and paints a picture of internal evils. It is stated that "the law is slacked [paralyzed, made useless] —judgments go forth perverted" (v. 4). The prophet could see his world coming down around him. The kingdom was crumbling before his eyes. Furthermore, deceitful men were taking advantage of the situation. Because of the chaos that existed, dishonesty prevailed and certain men exploited all they could for themselves. Habakkuk complains of the iniquity in verse 3: "for spoiling and violence are before me." In addition, in verse 4 he notes that the dignity and the rights of individuals were being ignored (the law was powerless).

As the moral integrity of men declined, the temptation to do wrong multiplied—even to the extent that those who desired good were swept along with the majority by the onrushing flood of social, commercial, political, and religious evils. "The wicked encompass the righteous" (v. 4). Those who resisted were finding the pressure too great and the persecution increasingly severe. There is no doubt that Habakkuk, too, was feeling the increasing pressure of evil. Perhaps it was his cries to God that kept him from being swept along like so many of his contemporaries.

What else can be said other than that Habakkuk was a desperate man? He found it difficult to be patient with God. He had prayed long and in earnest but no relief had come. His cry—"How long?"—was to be his last for, as far as he was concerned, help had to come soon or he, too, would be lost. His demise would soon come.

Habakkuk's cries are not new. They have risen from tired and troubled hearts of every generation. If you listen, you can hear them coming from the walls of Joseph's Egyptian prison or from the lips of Moses during his lonely hours when he brooded over the cruel tortures of God's people in bondage. They come from Daniel in the midst of the Babylonian captivity. They come from Jeremiah and Isaiah and even from Jesus who cried from the cross, "My God, my God, why have you forsaken me?" It is the age-old question asked again and again, "Why do the innocent suffer and the unrighteous prosper?" (see Ps. 73:12-14 and Jer. 5:28).

Today we hear it coming from an alienated and estranged humanity with its multitude of sin. It comes from a bleeding and tortured Vietnam, from a too long plundered Africa, and even from affluent America. Such is the case with the oppressed man who cries, "How long will it take for a man to be free?"—free to live in decent housing in a place of his choice, free to find satisfaction in a vocation that is fulfilling and without tokenism, free from all the prejudice passed from generation to generation, free to be the person God created him to be.

We can hear the cry of despair from the ghettos of our cities. Urban crisis after urban crisis has arisen and there is little release for the mass of humanity entangled in them. Even the most affluent area of suburbia cries out: "Is this all there is to life?"

If you walk down the corridors of our many hospitals, you will hear the same cry of despair from the rooms laden with the sick, the rejected, the lonely and forgotten. Our young people ask the same question. They see at times what we do not see or wish to ignore. They feel the effects of war; they hear the pain of hunger; they see injustice and prejudice. There is no generation gap with this question and the prophet speaks for all.

No man in the midst of life's activities can help but recognize that the conditions described by Habakkuk closely resemble those that are found in social, political, commercial, and even religious circles of our own day. An individual has to live in a vacuum or close off reality in order to ignore them. Our daily experiences certainly confirm the existence of those conditions. Tom Skinner, the black evangelist, in his book, *Words of Revolution,* reinforces this picture when he says:

Professionals from all walks of life are telling us that the human race is in trouble. Biologists, ecologists, psychologists, sociologists, economists and political experts are all united in this diagnosis of trouble . . . We've come to the place where human rights are no longer important; people are no longer important; lives are no longer important. Many of our young people are rebelling against the system because we have become a nation that worships the god of money and materialism. We are to the point where we are no longer committed to human rights.

What is the solution? Is there an answer? If we hear these hopeless cries or if we express them ourselves, do we simply give up or does God give us hope through Habakkuk's quest? We who live in such difficult times must walk the same path Habakkuk did. Walk that path with me.

This fact emerges—that man's main concern with the dark fact of suffering is not to find an explanation: it is to find a victory. It is not to elaborate a theory: it is to lay hold upon a power.

From *The Strong Name*
James S. Stewart

DISCUSSION QUESTIONS

First Session

1. How do today's conditions resemble those of Habakkuk's time? List the conditions you feel are similar and discuss their significance.
2. Who are the Habakkuks of our time? What reasons can you give for your choices?
3. Were there other eras in history reminiscent of Habakkuk's time? What were they and what was the result of their chaos?
4. Reread verses 1–4. Was Habakkuk's despair his reaction to the iniquity itself or was his despair from the effect that iniquity was having on his contemporaries? How have you felt in similar situations?
5. What made Habakkuk so desperate—his situation or his understanding of God and His activities among mankind?

Second Session

1. Is the cry of the Christian (the "why?" cry) different from the cry of the non-Christian? If so, why?
2. Does humanity—individually or as a nation—suffer hellish circumstances longer than necessary? Is this due to man's stubbornness and refusal to listen to God's Spirit?
3. In what ways has this form of suffering come to you? Be as honest in the discussion of this question as you can.
4. In what ways has this form of suffering come to your nation? Take a newspaper, giving each person a section, underlining what you feel is germane to the question, and share. What recent national and global

political situations contribute to your answer of this question?

5. How does the above list compare with the list of grievances in verses 2–4?

6. People make up a nation. In what ways do our hang-ups affect others, at the family-neighborhood level as well as at the national level?

Third Session

1. In the introduction are mentioned two contemporary novels which deal with issues of our time. Name at least two more recent works which, in your opinion, deal with similar issues. Share what you believe to be what they present as a solution.

2. If we believe God has a divine plan for us, is it right to question His plan? What right did Habakkuk have to question his God? Are there other occasions in the Bible where this has happened? Have you done this?

3. Must we regard situations that are unacceptable, such as poverty, war, famine, racial injustice, as being in God's plan? If not, why not?

4. Does God alienate people intentionally? Are there Scripture passages that seem to support this idea?

5. Have you felt the effect of evil in your own life? See verse 4.

God be in my head
And in my understanding.
God be in my eyes
And in my looking.
God be in my mouth
And in my speaking.
God be in my heart
And in my thinking.
God be at my end
And at my departing.

2. Habakkuk's First Vision
Habakkuk 1:5-17

God finally answers Habakkuk's cry and the solution comes in the form of a dream or a vision. In the first part of the vision a curtain is lifted to unfold the immediate future. It reveals the impending scourging of the land by the conquering Chaldeans* (Babylonians). Habakkuk is shocked at what he envisions. What is revealed is so unexpected, so inexplicable that he cannot believe it. The prophet becomes so disturbed that he dares to question God's will. Very few times do we encounter this in the Old Testament prophets, for they spoke out against evils and injustices, against idolatry and immorality; but seldom did they question God—their God.

The very thought that God would permit the cruel, covetous, besotted, idolatrous hordes of Chaldea to overwhelm His people seemed blasphemous and inconsistent with His dealings with Israel. Furthermore, for Habakkuk, this was a denial of the power as well as the justice and faithfulness of Jehovah. What a traumatic experience for the prophet! The first portion of the vision, which I call the "Impending Scourge," brought him no satisfaction. It only sent him into deeper depression. There was

*Scholars seem to think that this invasion took place sometime between 608 and 597 B.C.

no peace of mind. It seemed as if God had no answer for the present situation and no hope for the future. New burdens and new problems were added to the old. However, the prophet is not yet defeated, his fears have not overcome him yet, he still has enough courage to ask another question! "Wherefore?" (vv. 12–13):

> *Art thou not from everlasting, O Lord my God, mine Holy One? we shall not die. O Lord, thou hast ordained them for judgment; and, O mighty God, thou hast established them for correction. Thou art of purer eyes than to behold evil, and canst not look on iniquity: wherefore lookest thou upon them that deal treacherously, and holdest thy tongue when the wicked devoureth the man that is more righteous than he?*

Habakkuk's reaction is very human. When one is not satisfied with what he sees, it is his instinctive nature to ask another question in hope that more light will be shed on the situation. The glimpses we have of the future, being vague and incomplete, do not always help answer life's problems. There is a paradox here, for we often seek glimpses of the future in order that we may better understand the present and plan for the days to come. That's the kind of human beings we are.

If this were not the case thousands of people from all walks of life, from Park Avenue to the mountains of Tennessee would not need Jeane Dixon or the horoscopes that appear daily in the newspapers of the land. People would not be intrigued with the occult, or seek answers in so-called "white magic ritual." There is no doubt that we live in unusual times. Educated and uneducated alike are turning to the occult for some kind of direction and positive word for the future. An article appeared in *Time* magazine which stated:

> It is one of the stranger facts about the contemporary U.S. that Babylon's mystic conceptions of the universe are being taken up seriously and semi-seriously by the most scientifically sophisticated generation of young adults in history. Even the more occult arts of palmistry, numerology, fortune telling and witchcraft—traditionally the twilight zone of the undereducated and overanxious—are catching on with youngsters. Bookshops that cater to the trend are crammed with graduate students and associate professors.

I am convinced that people want to know what lies ahead because a moral sickness has developed in epidemic proportions and has caused a disintegration of personal relationships as well as a disenchantment with life and the world of which they are a part. As Habakkuk wanted order and answers, so too we want order in the universe and answers to our questions.

However, when such information is gained, if it is gained at all, it more often adds to, rather than helps solve, life's problems. In fact, experience teaches us that the glimpses we get of the future or its possibilities are among the chief causes of our frustrations and worries. The book *Future Shock* has been read by thousands, and science and technology in recent years have permitted us to see great possibilities, both good and bad. For example, we are all too aware of the fact that our earth is shortly going to be overpopulated and that a famine will strike before the end of the century. Some say that we have so polluted the air, lakes and streams that the process cannot be reversed. If this be true then the prospects of survival are nil.

Dr. Paul Ehrlich, Professor of Biology at Stanford University, has written a provocative book, *The Population Bomb*. It is based on three presuppositions: (1) too many people, (2) too little food, resulting in (3) a dying planet. He says:

> *I have just scratched the surface of the problem of environmental deterioration but . . . the causal chain of the deterioration is easily followed to its source. Too many cars, too many factories, too much detergent, too much pesticide, multiplying contrails, inadequate sewage treatment plants, too little water, too much carbon dioxide—all can be traced easily to too many people!*

Because of many medical and scientific breakthroughs we can now prolong life or destroy it. Atomic energy can produce enough power to maintain us or produce an atomic holocaust. We can use the sea to feed us or we can kill it. Dr. Bernard Ramm in *The Right, the Good, and the Happy* comments:

> *The truth of the matter is that if any scholar of one of the major scientific disciplines would ramble on with the expectations of the achievements of his branch of science in the future, we would all be breathless and stunned at the end of the discussion. The common man has no real sense or understanding of the kind of revolutionary things that are going to take place beginning in the near future.*

We can also find examples in the more common day-to-day problems of our society. Is it not true that we seek solutions regarding the crime that plagues us, the drug problem, alcoholism, the misuse of manpower, and the like? We are then shocked at the possible direction or answer. Take the problem of crime or law and order, for example. Did you know that crime in this land has really become an acceptable way of life, that crime has increased something like 119 per cent in the last ten years? The percentages are equally startling for other problems. We seek opinions, and the possible consequences fill us with more fear and apprehension. Why? What is wrong?

If we look more closely at Habakkuk's vision, we see that there is a similarity here. The trouble was not with the vision—it was clear enough. The trouble was with Habakkuk. He was unable to deal with what he saw, nor did he completely understand it. He could not comprehend what was being suggested in terms of God's providence. Unable to comprehend he was not in a position to let this aspect of God's sovereignty mature in his thinking process. As we study the book we can see the vision clearly. However, Habakkuk was too close to the event to comprehend the vision.

Too many procedures or objectives often prevent us from understanding God's dealings with His people. A reason for this is the fact that we live in the midst of action. Being "where the action is" is not always the best place to be. We are experiencing crisis—a situation which has become part of our existence. This being the case, often the problem becomes distorted and magnified out of shape and proportion. We see and experience but we cannot put the problem into its true perspective. Everything becomes a part of a great puzzle and too many pieces do not fit. All our experiences, all of life's encounters, do not seem to play a role in God's purpose or goals for humanity. We will not let God be God.

Jesus' disciples encountered a similar experience.

Long honored with Jesus' confidence concerning His death, they utterly failed to understand what it meant; and at the time of His trial, they were totally unprepared for what transpired. It was as if Christ had never spoken a word concerning the cross. As a matter of fact, we can hear Jesus pleading with the disciples, and finally saying, "I have many things to say but you are unable to bear them." Mark simply comments, "They understood not" (Mark 9:32).

Think of the implications here. With all the increased knowledge of our times, with the privileges of tremendous insight and hope beyond that of any other age, with the dreams of a better, greater society, we have little light to help us overcome the problems that exist. The heart of humanity cries out for more understanding, for more illumination on the dark things of life. For in spite of dreams and visions of how things can be, we repeat Habakkuk's question—"Wherefore?"

Unfortunately, man finds himself in a state of confusion and, as a result of his ignorance, his blindness, his utter failure to comprehend things as they are, he attempts to fill his life with the insignificant. Man tends to escape by surrounding his life with things—material possessions, what Paul describes as the "pleasures of this world." Individuals who engage in this form of escapism care little for, and see little of, God's activity in this world on behalf of mankind. Having only the frightening prospects of the future glaring before him, man will begin to look at the temporal things of life as the only reality—live for today and forget tomorrow. Jeremiah had a similar response: "There is no hope, but we will walk after our own devices and we will every one do the imagination of his evil heart" (18:12). In the end man will find himself a slave of evil and his heart will fail out of fear.

Humanity, with no vision or understanding of God's love and sovereignty, will die without faith and hope. The apostle Peter wrote in his second letter, "But whoever does not have [the Christian qualities] is so shortsighted that he cannot see, and has forgotten that his past sins have been washed away" (II Peter 1:9). According to Peter, such qualities produce a strong faith which is capable of sustaining an individual in the midst of life's tragedies or the unexpected. However, Peter goes a step further and suggests that such qualities give one hope for the future. However dark the clouds may be makes little difference. Can you not hear Peter saying, "Don't you remember who you are and what God has done?"

The qualities of life set forth by Peter are for all people who are willing to let the Lord of life control their whole being. Jesus Christ was sent by the Father to set men free, to "give us life and life more abundantly." Herein lies the secret of endurance. It is because of what Jesus Christ has done and will do that we can face all the cold facts of life with firmness and assurance.

So Habakkuk's experience, as well as that of many others, clearly indicates that human reflection on impending events is not only insufficient but discouraging and frustrating. If, then, our lives are to be directed, if we are to solve the problem the present holds, if we are to establish a satisfactory style of life, we must have help beyond that which even the most enlightened man can give. We must continue to walk the path with Habakkuk, see where he goes and what he does, and thus find help beyond ourselves.

Needless to say, ample confirmation of this is found in the multitudes who are making no effort to deal with life, no struggle, taking no steps against the evil of our time. They are the real silent majority who are afflicted with a virus called apathy. Indifference has affected too many. To be sure there are cries that are heard—the college student, the intellectual, the pacifist, the black man, the militant, poverty stricken individuals, and some Christians—but all too many men are silent. Too many have given up.

I remember something that happened in seminary which illustrates this. In one speech class we were learning how to deliver "children's sermons." A close friend had forgotten and come to class unprepared. So he decided to make up a story as he went along. When his time came he began to tell the story of a barnyard. All was peaceful and content in this yard. The horse ate with the mule and the duck with the pigs—life went on in a wonderful, joyful way. Then one day the farmer brought a new animal to the barnyard, a large overgrown bull. From that day on things just did not go right, all kinds of discouraging events took place. The chickens found their food eaten, there wasn't enough hay for the horses. The pigs had no water. Life became very difficult and unbearable. The animals were rather upset and soon found out that the bull was causing all the trouble. The bull had a problem: he didn't know how to get along or how to share life in the barnyard. Several animals went to him, but to no avail; he continued to live for self. As the story got longer and longer and my friend found it difficult to end it, he was in trouble and we all knew it. It became rather humorous. Finally he said, "And so the animals in the barnyard, not knowing what to do, or afraid to do anything, all lay down and died."

The class burst into laughter but after a moment or two a sobering thought hit us all. Without knowing it, he had given us a perfect example of apathy and defeatism.

We need more than anything else a knowledge that is beyond the power of our own reasoning. We need to be reminded of Habakkuk's suggestion: "I will watch to see what He will say to me" (2:1). It's not the answer, but the beginning of a pilgrimage.

DISCUSSION QUESTIONS

First Session

1. Have you ever questioned what God was doing? Share an event from your own life when that happened. How did you deal with it?
2. Does Habakkuk indicate a method of dealing with the questioning servant? See verses 14-17.
3. Habakkuk took issue with God's wisdom in using certain methods; so did Job (34:9). Do we?
4. Habakkuk struggled with apathy. Where is the apathy around you and in you? Has your spiritual growth been hindered by apathy?
5. Read II Peter 1:5-9. What qualities of the Christian life are listed? Discuss one that seems meaningful to each of you. What is the area of most difficulty?

Second Session

1. We would never admit to being wiser than God, but do we imply such wisdom in our intellectual analysis of our problems and their solutions?
2. Because we are often unable to keep a proper perspective on situations, we turn from God to other things for fulfillment. What are those things in your life? Do they come between you and God? Why? What can you do to change the situation?
3. Can human desire to know the future be termed a secular desire or can a Christian have the same desire? If so, why? What does Christ say about this desire?
4. If we are too close to an event to realistically understand God's intent, how can we best let God be God, allowing His will and purpose to work in and through us?
5. In actuality, was Habakkuk trying to change God's mind? If so, what is the evidence?

Third Session

1. Can you recall when a problem was best faced with "I will wait to see what He will say to me"? Did it work? Is it realistic to live out the Christian life with this attitude?
2. How would you react if you had received the vision Habakkuk received? What, if any, would be your plan of action? Is there Biblical guidance for your action?
3. Are dreams a form of precognition? If someone came up to you and said, "I have just had the weirdest dream," would you try to interpret it, laugh it off,

or ask him what he ate for supper last night? Can the Holy Spirit speak to us by means of dreams?

4. How did Habakkuk show his trust in God? Can you do the same?

5. Why are we at times unable to hear what God is saying to us? Share reasons from your own lives for your inability to discern what God is saying and discuss.

It is vanity to set thy love on that
        which speedily passeth away,
And not to hasten thither
        where everlasting joy abideth.

It is vanity to mind only this
        present life and not to foresee
        those things which are to come.

Thomas à Kempis

Stand ye in the ways, and see,
and ask for the old [ancient]
paths, where is the good way,
and walk therein, and ye shall
find rest for your souls.

Jeremiah 6:16

3. Habakkuk's Second Vision
Habakkuk 2

Someone once said, "God Almighty has help for all our human weaknesses and sin." If this be true, and I believe it is, we must continue with the prophet and see what the outcome will be. Habakkuk took a step of faith and said, "I will watch to see what He will say to me" (2:1).

What did the prophet do and what was the result of his action? First, Habakkuk went to what is commonly known as the "prayer tower" and there allowed God to communicate further with him. In essence, he would not allow all the depressing events of the day to diminish his desire to listen to God. He was still willing to trust even if that trust was somewhat weakened.

The end result of the watch was a second vision which is distinguished from the first vision in that the second was of the distant future while the first was of the immediate future. So far, we have encountered two visions in our study. Perhaps it would be appropriate at this point to make a few pertinent remarks. I think they need to be made before we proceed further in the study of the prophet.

Visions, as such, give us contemporary men a great deal of difficulty. This kind of spiritual experience is not normative for us. We severely resist experiences such as Habakkuk's, believing them to be far beyond our comprehension. For the most part, visions do not have a place in our religious consciousness, and we therefore regard Habakkuk's experience, or that of any of the other prophets, as less relevant than we should.

However, one thing cannot be denied. Christians have long recognized, even if they have only given lip service to the fact, that God's Spirit works in mysterious ways, that God will be God, and will choose how and when He will communicate with His people. If we examined the Scriptures carefully, we would be amazed how important visions are in the redemptive drama that unfolds. For example, the author of the Book of Hebrews states emphatically that "In the past God spoke to our ancestors many times and in many ways through the prophets, but in these last days He has spoken to us through His Son" (Heb. 1:1-2a).

Peter, in his Pentecost sermon, when attempting to share the unusual event of the upper room with the mystified public, quotes the prophet Joel:

Fellow Jews and all of you who live in Jerusalem, listen to me and let me tell you what this means. These men are not drunk as you suppose; it is only nine o'clock in the morning. Rather, this is what the prophet Joel spoke about. "This is what I will do in the last days, God says: I will pour out my Spirit upon all men. Your sons and your daughters will prophesy; your young men will see visions, and your old men will dream dreams. Yes, even on my slaves, both men and women, I will pour out my Spirit in those days, and they will prophesy. I will perform miracles in the sky above, and marvels on the earth below. There will be blood, and

*fire, and thick smoke; the sun will become dark,
and the moon red as blood, before the great and
glorious Day of the Lord arrives. And then, whoever calls on the name of the Lord will be saved"
(Acts 2:14-21).*

It is equally important to realize that Joseph, relying on
the dream or vision that God gave him, saved Christ
from the swords of Herod's soldiers and that Isaiah, the
prophet, as well as Jeremiah, were called to the prophetic
ministry by visions—one as he stood in the Temple and
the other as he walked in the garden. Furthermore, the
Book of Revelation is a vision given to John, and Zech-
ariah, the father of John the Baptist, had a visionary
experience in the Temple which announced the birth
of his son. It was such a moving experience that it shut
his mouth. To deny that God can and does communicate by means of visions, yesterday or today, denies His
sovereignty.

Here in chapter 2 God gives Habakkuk a second
chance to understand by means of a second vision—
a vision of things that will happen in the distant future,
which, if I am correct in my interpretation, moves us
not only through the history of Israel but right into the
New Testament and even to our own times and beyond.
This is the bright star in all his prophecy. This is the
underlying and significant factor—that the hope which
Habakkuk received in the vision is the same hope that
the Christian community maintains: that history, as
we know it, is in God's hands; it is God's story and He
is in control. This is what allowed Habakkuk to come
down out of the prayer tower and walk in the streets.
This is what kept Peter, James and John going. This

hope was at the very center of the New Testament church. Is this not what Jesus was teaching in Mark 13 and 14 and also in Matthew 24? Did He not reassure His disciples that the Father holds the future in His hands, and that even He, as the Son of God, must trust the Father? Careful examination of the record of the Ascension in Acts 1 shows that Luke is reassuring us with the same type of hope: that if the Father saw fit to send His Son, allowing Him to be put on a cross and then raising Him up from the dead, it is just as certain that He will return. It occurs to me that Jesus was given forty days to specifically prepare the disciples not only for their world-wide ministry but to reassure them that God the Father had one final act in history that He would perform. As Luke writes in Acts 1, "Men of Galilee, why do you stand looking up at the sky? This Jesus who is taken up from you into heaven will come back in the same way that you saw him go up into heaven."

It was this very aspect of the Christian faith upon which Paul depended. Again and again Paul reassures the Gentile church that, although things may seem dismal now, God will have the last word in history. If Habakkuk experienced this hope and if the early church leaders lived by it, then we, too, living in our time, need to live by it. Our hopes for the present are seen in our hope for the future—the future as God sees it.

God has a plan for the world, for every nation, for every people; and history, as we experience it, will end in God's time when all that He has decreed has been fulfilled. Many have described this as the "Blessed Hope" or the "Kingdom of God." Others have called it the "End Times," the "Kairos," or the "Fulfillment of

Time." Some Christians, including this author, believe that we are living in the End Times, that the End Times began with the Incarnation of Christ and will end with his second return. I think that Habakkuk's vision can be legitimately interpreted by the New Testament's concept of the Kairos.

However, let it be said that to do this creates two real dangers. These dangers have journeyed through the church for centuries. First, some Christians become too preoccupied with the Kairos, or End Times, and therefore are unable to see their present predicament. They can't really think through all the implications of life here and now, but view life only in terms of the tomorrow, or the "pie in the sky." On many occasions, I have heard this type of Christian saying, "Jesus is coming, Hallelujah, Amen. When He comes, all will be made right." The tragedy that occurs here is that this becomes a cop-out on life. It's a means of running away from the very things that Habakkuk was struggling with. Unfortunately, this kind of Christian is neither willing nor able to face the issues of his time. And, of course, dealing with the crises of his time is precisely what the Christian should do, especially in view of what Christ has done and in view of the Christian hope.

I am afraid for this kind of Christian because for him life is too difficult to cope with, too harsh to face. It is easier to dream or fantasize reality away. Francis A. Schaeffer in his booklet, "The New Super Spirituality" shares the same conviction:

> *Still another mark of the new super-spirituality is the emphasis on the spectacular and the extraordinary, and along with this the emphasis on an eschatology-centered theology. In evangelical*

circles in both England and America for perhaps the last ten or fifteen years, prophecy, eschatology, has been despised. It grew to be despised among the young biblical theologians because their parents had bickered over the smallest of eschatological points. In these older evangelical circles, somebody would suddenly lash out against somebody else because of a small shift in the program he promulgated. One said, "One, two, three, four," and another said, "One, two, four, three." And bang!— the war was on. The younger generation got sick and tired of it, and consequently in some of the theological seminaries where I have lectured there has been little interest in prophecy, in eschatology. Now, among many of the young, prophecy, rather than being a part of a larger whole of theology, has become the integration point of whatever theology they have. Eschatology has been blown up out of proportion. I hold very definite views on eschatology, but eschatology is not the integration point of my theology. I think that prophecy is often popular now just because of the current interest in all that is spectacular. The more extraordinary the better. Excitement is the thing. What is desired is the quick, easy solution. On both the non-Christian and the Christian side there is a kaleidoscope of rapidly changing fashions. What is sought is instant everything.

On the other hand, there is the second danger that because of such an overemphasis on a beautiful hope and doctrine some people will lay the eschatological aside completely, attempting to work in the world without the kind of hope that Habakkuk and the early church had. I have struggled with these very same problems, for

I was educated at two Christian colleges where there was too much emphasis on the "pie in the sky in the sweet by-and-by" and little on living life here and now. There was too much emphasis on how this is to take place— pre- or post-Rapture, pre- or post-Millenium. I wanted to forget the whole thing for a while and I did. But reading Habakkuk and the New Testament again reaffirmed my conviction that we must at one and the same time deal with the crises of the present world and keep our eyes on the eschatological. I am persuaded that we must proclaim the fact that the hope of the world rests in what Christ has done on the cross and in the promise of His return. Paul wrote in Ephesians 1:7-10:

For by the death of Christ we are set free, our sins are forgiven. How great is the grace of God which he gave to us in such large measure. In all his wisdom and insight God did what he had to, prepared and made known to us the secret plan he had already decided to complete by means of Christ. God's plan, which he will complete when the time is right, is to bring all creation together, everything in heaven and on earth, with Christ as Lord.

Paul is simply saying to us that "God is doing His thing in His time." This means that the present and the future do not belong to the political leader, to the economist, nor to the church, but to His Son, Jesus Christ.

It is in this aspect of the Christian faith that I put all my hopes and dreams, my despair and trials, because I know, like Habakkuk, that God is in control. My own denomination, the United Presbyterian Church, clearly states this in the Confession of 1967:

The life, death, resurrection, and promised coming

of Jesus Christ has set the pattern for the church's mission. His life as man involves the church in the common life of men. His service to men commits the church to work for every form of human well-being. His suffering makes the church sensitive to all the sufferings of mankind so that it sees the face of Christ in the faces of man in every kind of need. His crucifixion discloses to the church God's judgment on man's inhumanity to man and the awful consequences of its own complicity in injustice. In the power of the risen Christ and the hope of his coming the church sees the promise of God's renewal of man's life in society and of God's victory over all wrong.

This is what Habakkuk came to understand. When he experienced this kind of hope, when it became a part of his consiousness, he had no difficulty in accepting the vision. In contrast with the original vision in chapter 1, this second vision promised what he was looking for. In spite of the fact that the contents of the vision were for the distant future—"For the vision is yet for an appointed time, but at the end it shall speak and not lie. Though it tarry, wait for it, because it will surely come. It will not tarry" (2:3)—Habakkuk could live with this. This vision satisfied his longing for an answer. If it did nothing else, it satisfied his hunger for knowledge and understanding.

At this point, let us look at the vision more carefully, for by now you recognize that it was not given to an old man near death nor was it simply the folly or fancy of the prophet's imagination. It was, in all aspects of reality, a God-given view of plans already settled in redemptive history. Habakkuk, like John in exile on the isle of

Patmos, was chosen as a vessel in whom God could confide.

First, through the vision the prophet comes to understand that God is sovereign over all His creation; that is, He is the Lord of life and He has an ultimate plan for humanity. When Habakkuk understands this, then he is able to see wrongs corrected, justice administered, truth triumphant and, finally, the presence and power of God covering and transforming the earth. Coming like a cool breeze on a hot summer night, this knowledge gives Habakkuk new courage and strength, a faith and a quality of life to live by.

What is so important about this vision is the fact that Habakkuk saw the vision for us as well. In verse 2 he is commanded to "write the vision and make it plain on the tables that he may run that readeth it" (that he who reads may be a messenger of the vision).

This not only refers to the hope and plans of God in redemptive history, but it also has significance for our understanding of the five woes that are a part of the vision. These five woes attack the very foundation of the sin of the Chaldeans as well as the very foundation of sin committed by nations in any age.

Let us look for a moment at these woes. The first two woes are against individuals or nations who secure their material possessions or their riches by evil means (2:6-14). Habakkuk is told that God will have the final victory by allowing these individuals or nations to be destroyed by the very same means they use to destroy. "The very stones in the walls of your homes cry out against you and the beams in your ceilings echo what they say" (2:11). The third woe is against those who build cities or great metropolitan areas with money gained by crime, by exploitation, or by enslaving the populace and ignoring their needs. "Woe to you who build cities with money gained from murdering and robbery. Has not the Lord decreed that godless nations' gains will turn to ashes in their hands?" The fourth woe is against those individuals or nations that intentionally cause their neighbors to sin and then enjoy watching them suffer because of their sin. "Woe to you for making your neighboring lands reel and stagger like drunkards beneath your blows and then gloating over their nakedness and shame. ... You cut down the forests of Lebanon, now you will be cut down. You terrify the wild animals you caught in your traps; now terror will strike you because of all your murdering and violence in cities everywhere" (2:15-17). The final woe is against those who worship false gods. "Woe to those who command their lifeless wooden idols to rise and save them, who call out to the speechless stones to tell them what to do. Can your images speak for God? They are overlaid with gold and silver, but there is no breath at all inside" (2:19).

It seems to me that all of this points to the fact that God will have His way with men who do not honor Him, those who do not respect justice and righteousness, nor human dignity, those individuals who love darkness rather than light, evil rather than good, who have no pity nor conscience. Furthermore, it seems to me that these are warnings not only to the Chaldeans but to all nations and peoples. In our own times, I think it speaks clearly about the place of social reform in a land where there is so much hunger and injustice in the midst of great riches and material possessions.

Clearly, then, the vision is for humanity in every age. It is as relevant now as it was then. The Lord of life has not changed His plan. Redemptive history remains a part of God's action in the world. We still need the prophet's message and vision. Certainly it cannot be written off as the thinking of another age. If we do, we are playing into the hands of evil thinking and demonic forces. We must be aware that often the most discerning men cannot see how miserable and disheartening are present conditions, how discouraging are the prospects for survival. Even if we make allowance for every possible advancement in science, survival seems hopeless or, if not hopeless, very far out of reach.

Even Christ Himself spoke of the wheat and the tares growing together. He said that men's hearts would fail them from fear; that humanity would suffer a certain amount of tribulation, hardship, suffering, and death; that the love of men would wax cold (Matt. 24). If such words are true, can we hope for peace in this world? Yes, if we can see what Habakkuk offers.

What does the prophet have to say? Is there something in the second vision which gives direction and hope —hope which does not lead us to cop out on life? Is there something which will help us to deal with the circumstances of life? Yes, and it is this. Habakkuk comes face to face with hope for the future. Because of this hope we, too, can hear the God of Creation declaring, "The day of the Lord will come." "In due season ye shall reap if ye faint not." This is the answer. God assures us, like Habakkuk, that all these dark things, these inexplicable events of our own day, the realities we must all face, work out the counsels of His own will. Furthermore, they are "working together for good to them that love him." Though it is not explicit, as we can see from this side of the cross, there is the suggestion in Habakkuk

that Christ will come with power and glory as the Victor
of life and that with His coming will occur the destruction of evil that so entangles the human heart. There will
come a time when there will be no pain, no sighing,
no crying; when death will cease to exist and its sting
will be destroyed. I suggest that this is the significance
of the vision, for Habakkuk declares, "The Lord is in
His holy temple; let all the earth keep silence before
Him" (2:20).

DISCUSSION QUESTIONS

First Session

1. In what different ways does God communicate with
   His people? Does God continue to communicate
   today?
2. What is the hope mentioned in the Scriptures? What
   understanding of hope do you have?
3. What is the "second vision"?
4. What is God's plan in the "fullness of time"?
5. What is the difference between hope in Christ and re-
   signing oneself to the will of God?
6. How does all of this affect your life as a Christian?

Second Session

1. "He who lives by the sword dies by the sword."
   Habakkuk saw evil people destroyed by the forces
   they were using. Today that could be nuclear power;
   radioactive fallout could contaminate the strato-

sphere, encircling the globe and eventually killing or causing mutations in all life. What does his vision mean today?

2. The statistics on crime, especially in metropolitan areas, are increasing out of all proportion to the population growth. Large areas are relying more and more on federal funds in order to continue operations for basic services such as police, fire protection, sanitary precautions (including salaries for garbage collectors). Can this be part of the second woe of Habakkuk coming true today?

3. What are the false gods of today?

4. Can you cite any recent action of the American government that might put the United States in the category of those nations that intentionally cause their neighbors to sin and then enjoy watching them suffer because of their sin? Is our international image one of a Christian country in the real sense of the word? Discuss.

5. The 1950s and 1960s were a time of great technological advancement. Could the 70s and 80s be one of spiritual advancement? If so, why?

Third Session

1. Does the wickedness of the Chaldeans expose the kind of gods they worshiped?

2. If we should be trodden down by communism, could the following gods that we sometimes worship above God rise up and save us: knowledge, materialism, popularity, family closeness, status, good works, acceptance by those around us, food, comfort?

3. In countries suffering extreme poverty and famine, wooden gods, Buddhas, animals, gurus, etc., are worshiped on a massive scale while Christianity is strongly rejected. Is it fair to blame God for the suffering of those who will not open when He knocks?

4. Do you think this finite world of men will ever become the Kingdom of God on earth? If not, why not? What support do you find in the Scriptures?

5. "The Lord is in his holy temple; let all the earth keep silence before him" (v. 20). Anything that we really want to do, we'll practice until we perfect it. How can we practice worship and silence before a holy God?

This is my Father's world,
O let me ne'er forget
That though the wrong seems oft so strong,
God is the Ruler yet.

This is my Father's world:
The battle is not done;
Jesus who died shall be satisfied,
And earth and heaven be one.

Maltbie D. Babcock (1858-1901)

The primary proposition of
the Christian, his ultimate act
of faith, is the trustworthiness
of Jesus Christ.

D. Elton Trueblood
A Place to Stand

4. Habakkuk's Victory
Habakkuk 2, 3

All that has been said in the closing portion of the previous chapter may be true and all of what Habakkuk implies about the future may be correct, but we are still faced with the age-old problem, "Lord, I believe, help my unbelief." Present conditions in the world continue to force doubt and fear to the forefront of our thoughts. Many people stand in the dark shadows of life and cry, "Lord, how long can I wait for this? Is there no help now?"

It is a legitimate question and unless we can answer it in a manner clearly understood by all, two things happen. On the one hand, those who cannot accept the second coming of Christ as a valid aspect of the faith will walk away saying, "It's just a bunch of religious hogwash; we need something for now. Don't tell me what will be some day."

On the other hand, those who can understand this hope will rely on it too much and enter into a form of "eschatological escapism." Many Christians have consciously and unconsciously fallen into this trap. They express the thought that nothing can be done now to see the situation clearly—thus, "Let us put our trust in the 'pie in the sky'—remember, Jesus is coming!"

In my view, this is heretical because the hope that

Habakkuk speaks of is a hope with purpose, a hope which conditions and influences the present and does not escape from it. It does not involve being so heavenly-minded that one is of no earthly good.

The man who has helped me the most to understand this is Dr. Walter Rauschenbush, the nineteenth-century social reformer and theologian. In his book, *Christianity and the Social Crisis,* he talks about the social impetus of the early church and how the "blessed hope" influenced the early Christian community. He says, "A perfect religious hope must include both eternal life for the individual and the kingdom of God for humanity." Leighton Ford, in his book, *One Way to Change the World,* is saying the same thing to our generation:

> *This hope of Christ's return is no escapist clause, it is not an out for Christian complacency, nor an alibi for non-involvement. On the contrary, it is a spur to holiness, to evangelism, to obedience. It is a motivation to make God's work on earth our own. . . . Once God invaded history in Jesus Christ to begin His revolution. Some day, perhaps sooner than we think, He will intervene and bring His revolution to completion, making all things new. . . . In this interim period we are called to repent and believe the Gospel, to follow Jesus, our revolutionary leader, to preach His good news and practice new life.*

There is much more in Habakkuk than holding on to an event in history that will some day happen, important though that is. Habakkuk shares three principles of life, which he came to believe, three principles which changed the course of his life. What I am talking about is revealed in the statement: "The just shall live by faith" (2:4). This is Habakkuk's solution, his prescription for living the Christian life here and now. An understanding of this principle will give one direction and needed support. I am convinced that if we are going to come to an understanding of God's dealings with men and if we are to establish a lifestyle compatible with the times, then we must begin with *faith* as the foundation.

For the first time in the Old Testament we have explicitly expressed the impetus of Old Testament life, a requirement which God has always demanded, namely that men live out their lives on earth by faith.

The word for faith used by Habakkuk is *emuna,* which in Hebrew refers to the faithfulness of God. We do not create the faith, but trust completely in the One who is Creator and Sustainer of life. When the Septuagint version of the Old Testament translated the Hebrew into Greek, the significance of this was clearly understood by the scholars, for *emuna* was translated *pistis. Pistis* in Greek means the trustworthiness of God. Habakkuk teaches us that a life of faith is lived in the here and now—with all its problems and tensions—by depending on the faithfulness and reliability of God, and not on man or man's skills.

The apostle Paul picks up this theme in his Epistle to the Romans. Like the prophet, Paul had lost all confidence in his own ability as well as the abilities of others to correct matters. Both had given up in the struggle, and were ready to listen to what God wanted to do and say. This is the very thing that God requires of us and it is the very thing we resist. The Lord God said, "Be still and know I am God."

It would seem that God at this point was waiting for

Habakkuk, just as Habakkuk was waiting for God. Does this not suggest that until man loses all confidence in purely human efforts to correct matters and to create his own self-righteousness, he cannot put this principle of faith to work in his life? Sam Shoemaker, that great witness to the faith, said in his book, *Extraordinary Living for Ordinary Men:*

> Let us face at the outset how many Christians are not victorious, but defeated. Defeated by circumstances, defeated by other peoples' nature and wrongdoings, defeated by the down-drag of the flesh, defeated by loss, by pain, by suffering, by worry. Instead of saying with confidence, "This is the victory that overcometh the world, even our faith," they have to say in honesty, "This is the defeat that has been caused by the world, even our self-centeredness." That is the opposite of faith; self-centeredness is — being centered in self rather than in God. When I see people who pray the Lord's Prayer, who come to church, and who profess the faith, but who meet the difficulties of this life in just the same way as everybody else, with the same bitterness, the same petulant cry of "why?", the same demand of their rights, the same going down under sorrow, I know that there are many Christians in name who have never got above the lowlands of self-centered living, who have never gone up on the heights of faith, and there found victory in Christ which He is waiting to give them. But those heights are there, waiting to be climbed in faith.

So you see every Christian must learn this lesson over and over again. Failure in Christian living; failure to stand firm in the difficult areas of life; failure to correct injustice, to help the poor, to stop war; failure to learn how to love, how to relate and build wholesome relations —all indicate that we have neglected to apply this first principle.

The answer Habakkuk received does not call for Christians to escape life, but to be victorious over it, to be involved in it, and most important, to develop a lifestyle that is rooted in faith—the kind of faith which is sufficient to deal with the issues and to lift an individual out of despair into hope. Senator Mark Hatfield said it best in his book, *Conflict and Conscience:* "It is hypocritical for a Christian to claim he has the peace of God in his heart if he remains oblivious to the violence and destruction in the world."

The problem as I see it is that Christians too often think that this Christian life can be lived by their own vain efforts. Believing this to be true only leads to despair, and despair to apathy. Another prophet made a most relevant comment for the Christian of our times, "Not by might, nor power but by my Spirit, saith the Lord" (Zech. 4:6).

If we permit ourselves to fall into this trap and listen to the inner voices which are negative and discouraging, we will soon settle down into the ways of hopeless men who say, "Under the conditions in which I find myself, Christian living is impossible and intolerable." If you seem to be moving in that direction, hear the words of Habakkuk, "The just shall live by faith."

Let's take a step backward in order to take another step forward. I want to examine the concept of living out life by faith a little further. There is no doubt in my mind that living out life by faith is at the heart of Christ's message and the very center of all that the apostle Paul writes. It was William Barclay who said, "We only have to read his letters to see that for Paul the word 'faith' sums up the very essence of Christianity."

Paul quotes Habakkuk in Romans 1:17 and picks the topic up again in Galatians 3, when he deals with the legalistic problem of the Galatian church. And if Paul is the author of the Epistle to the Hebrews, he gives additional insight into faith in Hebrews 10 and 11.

In Romans Paul deals with the state of our existence. "All men have sinned and are far away from God's saving presence " (3:23). But the major theme is what God does for us. "For sin pays its wage—death; but God's free gift is eternal life in union with Christ Jesus our Lord" (6:23). It is in this context that Paul can write Habakkuk's words. "For the gospel reveals how God puts men right with himself: it is through faith alone, from beginning to end. As the scripture says, 'He who is put right with God through faith shall live' " (1:17). Or again, "God puts men right through their faith in Jesus Christ. God does this to all who believe in Christ" (3:26).

So in Romans it is made clear that we can have a new existence—by faith we can have a new lifestyle.

In Galatians we are encouraged to live out this life of faith in the freedom we find in Christ, rather than to adhere to the Old Testament law. This is seen clearly in Paul's statement in Galatians 2:16, "We know that a man is put right with God only through faith in Jesus Christ, never by doing what the Law requires." The word "put right" (also translated "justified") shows that God treats us as if the sin did not happen. Therefore we are free to be His people—servants of God, accepted just as we are. He welcomes us with no strings attached if we will only respond to that love.

However, I think there is a warning made clear in Hebrews where it is stated: "Now the just shall live by faith, but if any man turn back, my soul shall have no pleasure in him" or in the TEV: "My righteous people, however, will believe and live but if any of them turn back, I will not be pleased with him" (10:38).

I think this is directed to the people of God who, because of conditions around them, tend to turn back and give up. It is a warning to be faithful, to be loyal even during times of waiting and stress. The sentence which follows says: "We are not people who turn back and are lost. Instead, we have faith and are saved" (10:39).

There comes a day when we must trust God to be God. We may not see signs of life, but God is not dead. On the contrary, it is Jesus Christ, God's Son, and His provision for hope that keep the world from destroying itself.

I often read a passage in Paul's second letter to the Thessalonians which was meaningless to me until I could see that Paul in effect was saying: "The most important thing is to be faithful. For it is the Spirit of God that holds things together in this world. The mysterious wickedness is already at work, but what is going to happen will not happen until the one who holds it back is taken out of the way" (II Thess. 1:5-7). I believe Christ, through Paul, is telling us, "Trust me, not yourselves, and you shall live."

Habakkuk discovered this as did Paul. That is why Paul could write, "This life that I live now, I live by faith in the Son of God, who loved me and gave his life for me" (Gal. 2:20b).

To understand Paul's faith in the light of Habakkuk is important. Faith is seeing all that God does for us in His Son, Jesus Christ. As Barclay puts it, "Faith is the total assent of a man's total being to Jesus Christ. . . . Faith is the response of trust of a man's total personality to the love of God as shown us in the life and death of Jesus Christ."

To you who at this moment in history are discouraged by what you see and who are ready to forsake the Christ who loves you and the faith that has given you hope, I call upon you to take a second look, to experience a second touch. For faith in the living Christ does bring strength for your needs. Daring to live a life of faith will bring the secret of happiness to your total being and enable you to be an effective servant of God and man.

Recall the words of the old Irish folk tune, "Be Thou My Vision":

Be Thou my Vision, O Lord of my heart;
Nought be all else to me, save that Thou art —
Thou my best thought, by day or by night,
Waking or sleeping, Thy presence my light.

Be Thou my Wisdom, and Thou my true Word;
I ever with Thee and Thou with me, Lord;
Thou my great Father, I Thy true son;
Thou in me dwelling, and I with Thee one.

That's what it's all about!

We have a second principle in Habakkuk for the Christian life style. It is revealed in the words of chapter 2, verse 20, "The Lord is in His holy temple; let all the earth keep silence before Him." The second principle is to learn the discipline of silence before God. Simply stated, it means taking time out of the complex and busy schedule we set for ourselves to listen to what God is saying. We don't have to become a mystic to do this but, like Habakkuk, it is necessary for us to realize that no matter how thick the cloud that hides God from man, it remains true that the Lord is in His holy temple. Symbolically, the temple represents the universe—all of creation—of which God is in control. Habakkuk is reaffirming that God remains the Being behind all of life, and humanity must learn to be silent before Him.

I think it matters little whether we understand Habakkuk's utterance as a command or as an invitation. The prophet may either be calling on all the voices of the earth for silence because he is determined to hear what God is saying, or he may be calling on the people whose voices make up the babbling to share in the peace which he has now found by being silent before God. In either case, the fact remains the same. Habakkuk is testifying from personal experience that this second principle is of great importance. He has turned from the demonic voices which destroy faith to the liberating voice of the Almighty. This reminds us of Paul, who in the midst of the ever-increasing storm was able to find rest to which others were strangers. Listening to the still, small voice rather than the tempest, Paul could look at the world and all of its troubles and confess, "I believe, God, that it shall be even as it was told me" (Acts 27:25b).

I saw a sign on a car the other day which read: "Jesus— the bridge over troubled waters." That's another way to express it. When a man listens to God and trusts in Him, when he realizes that God's judgments are unsearchable and His ways past finding out, that all things are of Him and through Him, and that He who is on the throne is doing all things well, then man's complaining and questioning will cease. Such individuals are needed today, individuals who can say with Christ, "Even so, Father, for so it seemeth good in Thy sight—not my will but Your will be done." Habakkuk moved from being a questioning servant to a submissive servant.

We have examined the first two principles, *faith* and *silence*. Habakkuk confesses, "I will rejoice in the Lord, I will rejoice in the God of my salvation" (3:18). The third principle then is *peace*. There are great depths to the Christian style of life, but it is not enough for a man to have a vision from God, or even to understand the purposes of God. It is not enough that a man come to trust God and to have the power to live a life of faith and action. It is not enough that a man should know that even in the dark moments of despair God is not dead, but a living, vital force. It is not enough to be silent before Him. There is another aspect to life if we are to live a full, mature Christian life. Habakkuk realized it and Jesus taught it. One must have peace and joy. The gospel must set a man completely free. Look at what Christ taught. In John 14, Jesus offers His disciples peace. "Peace I leave with you, my peace I give unto you . . ." (v. 27). In John 15 Jesus promises His disciples joy. "These things have I spoken unto you, that my joy might remain in you, and that your joy might be full" (v. 11). Peace and joy are definitely a part of the gospel and the quality of a Christian life.

Let me take you a step further. Paul wrote in Romans 14:17, "The Kingdom of God is righteousness, peace and joy in the Holy Spirit." What does this mean? It means that peace and joy are the height, the final principle to which our God would have us come. We can experience life as Christ wanted us to when we know the peace and joy of the Lord. This is accomplished by letting the Spirit of God work in and through us.

The frustration I see on faces of Christians today comes from a lack of dependence of the Holy Spirit to give peace and joy. Habakkuk tells us that he had to come to such a point in his life. Here was a man who trusted God and even submitted to God, but he had to know something more than the mere purposes of God. He had to come to know God and to enjoy the peace and joy that He gives. He had to stop worrying about the problems of life and experience the solution to life. He was looking at the problems and not the possibilities. He had to become occupied with the Giver of life. Perhaps, in our contemporary terms, he had to come to be a whole person—he had to come to terms with himself and found his place in the scheme of faith in the midst of all the chaos. The peace of God became a part of Habakkuk's life.

I think this is the theme or thrust of the entire third chapter. The subject is God, the God who now is more to him than his questions, even more significant than the visions. God embraces Habakkuk and the prophet communes with Him.

His life took on a new perspective. He became satisfied and wrote on confession of faith:

Although the fig tree shall not blossom, neither shall fruit be in the vines; the labor of the olive shall fail, and the fields shall yield no meat; the flock shall be cut off from the fold, and there shall be no herd in the stalls: Yet I will rejoice in the Lord, I will joy in the God of my salvation. The Lord God is my strength, and he will make my feet

like hinds' feet and he will make me to walk upon
mine high places (3:17-19a).

What a beautiful thing! This was no idle boast. It
was the song of one who had become more than a con-
queror through the Lord that loved him. Don't forget
that there was no change in the conditions that previously
seemed unbearable. Conditions remained the same, but
the victory over those conditions was so great that the
prophet could say with confidence:

Though conditions wax worse and worse to the very
worst, my new found joy will not be touched or
tinged, for my joy is now in the Lord and not in
things.

(Author's paraphrase)

This is "where it is at" for Christians. Habakkuk's experience was also Jesus' experience. With foes haunting
Him, with friends forsaking Him, with death facing Him,
He could offer to share God's joy with His perplexed
friends and a troubled humanity. That, my friends, is
God's way, offering us life and life more abundant.
Again Paul, through Christ living in him, could sustain
the loss of all things and the suffering of great pain and
could make his prison cell ring at midnight with his song
of peace and joy. Those who rejoice in Christ know the
peace of God. Those who make Christ the object of their
lives are conquerors of life.

Dietrich Bonhoeffer wrote from prison:

[God] must be found at the centre of life. . . .
Christ is the centre of life, and in no sense did he
come to answer our unsolved problems. From the
centre of life certain questions are seen to be wholly

irrelevant, and so are the answers commonly given
to them — I am thinking for example of the judg-
ment pronounced on the friends of Job. In Christ
there are no Christian problems.

So Habakkuk, the prophet of old, with conditions unchanged, passed from the cry, "How long?" to a song of triumph, to a life fulfilled. We watch him go step by step from despair to knowledge, from knowledge to trust, from trust to submission, from submission to peace —the peace of the living God. So it is with many of God's people. Saul, the persecutor, became Paul, the proclaimer of Christ. Like Peter, confused and bewildered by what Christ did and said, when he was set right and made free, Paul could strengthen others. When men are confronted and helped by God, they comfort and help others. When the power of Christ's cross and the freedom of the Resurrection enter a life, that life is set free to right the wrong and to help make this world a fit place to live.

Oppressed people of America, fight for your rights, but know, too, the joy of Christ. City dweller, struggle for your humanity, but know also the joy of Christ. Plundered, chaotic world, struggle to be free, but know the joy of Christ. Know that God is in control—this world is His creation. All of us must take the path of Habakkuk from darkness to light.

I raised eyes aloft, and I beheld the scattered chapters of the universe gathered and bound into a single book by the austere and tender hand of God.

From The Divine Comedy
Dante (1265-1321)

DISCUSSION QUESTIONS

First Session

1. What is faith? Discuss what faith means to each of you.
2. We are called to depend on the faithfulness and reliability of God. What does He promise for today?
3. How does living by faith differ from your way of living? Do you live by faith?
4. What has Christ done for us beyond the "once and for all salvation"?
5. What is your response to Christ? What meaning does Jesus Christ have in your life?

Second Session

1. How did Habakkuk finally come to peace with God?
2. Do we have the responsibility as Christians to stand firm in difficult situations?
3. Where does one get the power to live by faith?
4. Habakkuk did not have the New Testament revelation that Paul had. Was Habakkuk's faith as great as Paul's?

5. How do you relate to Habakkuk? Can you apply his principles to your Christian life style? How?

Third Session

1. Many people live lives of service to humanity and do not know or acknowledge Christ, or even God. Is God working His will, His plan, through these people? What support from Scripture do you have for your answer?
2. Does Habakkuk give a solution for apathy?
3. What are some of the characteristics of God that might instill peace in our hearts?
4. Is it really possible to have peace in the midst of extreme suffering? See verses 17-18.
5. "Faith comes by hearing, and hearing by the Word of God" (Rom. 10:17). If Scriptural faith is worth having, why do so few people have it in good measure?
6. "I will joy in the God of my salvation" (Hab. 3:18b). What is the difference between joy and happiness?

Last Session

1. Habakkuk concludes his writing by saying that "the Lord God is my strength, and he will make my feet like hinds' feet and he will make me to walk upon mine high places" (3:19a). How can that be interpreted for you personally and for our social, political and spiritual leaders?
2. You have studied the message of this prophet. In what ways can you be Christ's servants in our time? What effect has this study had on you?